The 'op' Hop

By Viola & Zaida Stefano

VeeZee Publications

Copyright © VeeZee Publications Pty. Ltd. 2025
First published in Australia in 2025
by VeeZee Publications Pty. Ltd.
veezeepublications.com

The right of Viola Stefano to be identified as the author of this work have been asserted by her in accordance with the **Copyright Amendment (Moral Rights) Act 2000.**

All rights reserved. Apart from any use as permitted by the author & under the **Copyright Act 1968**, no part may be reproduced, copied, scanned, stored in a retrieval system, recorded, or shared, by any means or in any form, without prior written & signed authorization from the publisher.

ISBN: 978-1-923120-20-4

A catalogue record of this book is available from the **National Library of Australia.**

Author: Viola Stefano
Illustrations, cover & internal designs: Zaida Stefano

Illustrations copyright © Zaida Stefano 2025
Design copyright © Zaida Stefano 2025

Disclaimer: The content presented in this book is meant for educational purposes only. The author & publisher claim no accountability to any entity or person for any liability, damage, or loss caused or assumed to be caused directly or indirectly as a consequence of the application, use, or interpretation of the material in this book.

Core words used in this book

I	want	can	**stop**	**look**
like	**more**	he	**go**	see
here	what	**do**	**the**	**and**
out	where	we	it	**up**
not	**they**	when	**that**	**down**
she	now	**them**	is	put
help	off	**you**	yes	**on**
turn	who	this	no	why
done	make	a	to	under
come	in	some	which	**there**
open	get	good	same	home

Look at the frog hop.

Hop up there frog, hop.

Look at the mop, frog.

Hop on top of that mop.

Stop frog, stop.

There are bubbles

on the mop.

Look at them go

pop, pop, pop!

Just like you go hop, hop, hop!

Hop and pop, and down they go.

The frog and that mop are on the floor!

Do not hop, frog! Stop, more bubbles will pop.

Words that end in 'op' in this book

hop	pop	top
stop	mop	

Words with 'o' in this book

frog	not	on

We hope you had fun reading!

Learning made easy with VeeZee

VeeZee Publications

Wait, there's more!

Visit our website for information about our range of readers
& supporting products.

veezeepublications.com

www.ingramcontent.com/pod-product-compliance
Lightning Source LLC
Chambersburg PA
CBHW040301100526
44584CB00004BA/305